FOR YOU, LOVE ME
LIVING WITH AUTISM AND ADHD

KELLIE-ANNE GALLAGHER

For You, Love Me: Living with Autism and ADHD

By Kellie-Anne Gallagher

© 2024 Kellie-Anne Gallagher

Hembury Books

Ebook ISBN 9781763583665

Paperback ISBN 9781763583672

All rights reserved. No portion of this book may be reproduced in any form without permission from the author and publisher, except as permitted by Australian copyright law.

ABOUT THE AUTHOR

A dedicated mother, wife, and entrepreneur, Kellie-Anne Gallagher's life has been marked by a series of profound challenges and transformative experiences. These events have shaped her into a resilient and passionate advocate for neurodiversity.

Kellie-Anne masked the symptoms of stage four endometriosis for much of her life. The turning point came in 2017 when she faced a near-death experience due to a post-operative infection following a surgery to manage the condition.

This life-threatening ordeal forced her to confront her deepest fears and promise herself that she would survive and thrive—for herself and her son, Lucas Junior. This moment marked the beginning of a profound journey of self-discovery and spiritual awakening.

When her son, Lucas Junior, was diagnosed with ADHD and OCD at the age of 7, Kellie-Anne recognized her own experiences mirrored in his. This realization led to her own diagnosis of ADHD and a deeper understanding of her neurodivergent traits.

Diagnosed at the age of 39 with ADHD, autism spectrum disorder (ASD), anxiety, PTSD, and premenstrual dysphoric disorder (PMDD), Kellie-Anne has embarked on a journey of self-discovery and acceptance, transforming her challenges into opportunities for growth and deeper self-awareness.

Kellie-Anne and her husband, Lucas Senior—the love of her life—run a successful cabinet making business on the Gold Coast.

Together, they share their life with their 'miracle baby,' Lucas Junior, and their two cherished fur babies, Ronnie and Ruby.

Through her writing and advocacy, Kellie-Anne Gallagher hopes to offer support and solidarity to others navigating similar paths, and highlighting the strength and beauty that can be found in embracing one's true self.

📷 instagram.com/kellieannegallagher

For my son,
This book is for you. It's a guide to help you navigate this amazing, wild, beautiful ride called life as a neurodivergent.
This is my legacy to leave to you. You are sitting on the floor watching Sunday National Rugby League as I type this. You are only nine years old with so much living to do. My inspiration for this book is that we both have attention deficit hyperactivity disorder, or ADHD, so I know that you don't want to sit down and listen to me rattle on with all my 'parental knowledge'. So, I wrote you this book, so you can refer to it when you are ready in your time. Because everything comes to us at the right time when we need it. Life will have its ups and downs; its lessons and its blessings. Your father and I are here for you whenever you need us. Please remember you are always loved, and everything always works out in the end.
I love you in this life and the next.

To everyone else reading this book,
I wrote this with neurodivergent people like me in mind. We like things direct and to the point. So, readers, my book is short and sweet.
Nothing happens by chance. You found this book for a reason. It has been written to you with love and the intention of helping anyone who needs to hear my message.
May your life be filled with love, may you live your life to the fullest, learn all your lessons and receive countless blessings.
Love, me.

The stars in the sky are there to remind us there is something greater than the small space we are in, have faith things will get better and know you are divinely loved, guided and protected.
  - Kellie-Anne Gallagher

ABOUT ME, MY AUTISM AND MY ADHD

I'm so nervous about sharing this as it's deeply personal and leaves me open to a world of judgement. But I am sharing it because I wish someone was as open and honest about their experience as a neurodivergent person as I'm about to be, so that I didn't feel as alone and lost with the deep feelings I was experiencing.

I was diagnosed with ADHD, autism spectrum disorder (ASD), premenstrual dysphoric disorder (PMDD) and dyscalculia in 2023, when I was 39 years old. The day I was diagnosed was the day my life made sense.

You see, I spent my whole life up until that day knowing something was 'wrong' with me and that I was 'different'. I didn't know what it was. All I knew was things that were easy for everyone else were like walking through quicksand to me. To function in a world where things were so easy for others and hard for me meant my anxiety, my drive to succeed and my will to be the best I could be helped me function enough to get through.

I can be extremely self-critical; my inner dialogue can be awful. 'You're weird', 'you're too loud', 'you talk too much', 'you're stupid', 'you don't try hard enough', 'get over it', 'focus', 'stop daydreaming', 'apply yourself more' are all things I repeat to myself daily. But I repeat these because they were all the things I was told when I was a little girl.

I remember crying in maths class, telling my teacher, 'this is too hard, I don't get it'. I was told to focus more. When I was doing homework with my parents and I just couldn't understand the concept of mathematical equations that were so simple for them, I was told I need to focus more in class and apply myself more, because how could I not know how to do it, it's the easiest equation ever.

I learnt to play the violin by ear because I couldn't read music. I was too terrified to admit to my very strict teacher that I still didn't understand what notes meant, even after he had explained it to me five times.

Then, as an adult, doing the bookkeeping for our business (bookkeeping is all about numbers), I mentioned to my husband that I think I have a learning difficulty. He said in disbelief, 'there's no way you have a learning difficulty, you're one of the smartest women I know'. But that was just testament to how good I had become at 'masking', or hiding my difficulties, because no one thought girls could have ADHD.

People come into your life as lessons or blessings. One blessing goes by the name of Mrs Schumacher, my son's Year 2 teacher.

I have only one child and I hadn't been around many young children before I had my son. As a first-time parent, I had nothing to compare his behaviour to. From birth my son was confident, loud, energetic, always on the move, loving to chat and loving to try new things (the opposite of me).

He threw a lot of tantrums. I mean a *lot*. If we left somewhere and he was having fun and didn't want to go, he would lose it, to the point of hysterical crying, screaming and thrashing, and nothing and no one could calm him. His father and I would have to sit in the car and wait for it to pass. I put this down to his love of fun and not wanting to leave.

As he got older and became way better at communicating, the tantrums became fewer, more of a weekly rather than a daily occurrence. But his smartass and oppositional behaviour nearly made me lose my mind. I know he didn't mean it; I could tell it was an automatic comeback without maliciousness, but I would often be in disbelief, thinking *what the heck*.

In Prep he was one of the smart children who showed initiative, but he had freedom to run and play, and learning was more play-based. Grade 1 was a lot different. More was expected of him and he had to try to regulate his enthusiastic outbursts, his constant movement. There was less playing and more sitting. He was in trouble at school a lot.

By Grade 2, he started to notice that other kids could sit still and pay attention, and that he was in trouble the most often. One afternoon when he got home from school he lost it and had a meltdown over something, and I put him in his room to cool down. When I went in to check on him once he had calmed down, he turned to me and said, 'I am the stupidest kid ever, I am so dumb. I hate myself'.

It was like he had hit me with a brick. I was in shock. I had never discussed or told him about my inner dialogue, and here was my seven-year-old son speaking about himself in the same way I spoke to myself.

I wanted better. I wanted him to feel better about himself, so how could this be his default mentality when I actively tried so hard for it not to be?

That same week Mrs Schumacher pulled me aside and wanted to discuss some things about his performance at school. So we had a parent–teacher interview. In that interview she said, 'I have been noticing some behaviours, some lack of regulation'. She spoke in a way that alluded to ADHD without saying it. I straight out asked her, 'Do you think he has ADHD?', and she said, 'It's not for me to say, but let's do some further investigations'.

I walked out of that meeting and got straight on the phone and booked him in to see a child psychologist.

Mrs Schumacher's genuine care and love for her students and her not wanting to label him as the 'naughty kid' so he would be lost in the system and cast aside, not wanting to label him as 'difficult' or put him in the too-hard basket as many undiagnosed ADHD kids are, led to his diagnosis. I believe it has changed the course of his life for the better.

My son, Lucas, was diagnosed with obsessive-compulsive disorder (OCD), ADHD and anxiety. Finally, we could understand why regulating his emotions was so hard for him, why he constantly needed to move, why he lacked impulse control and needed to repeat particular movements. It became clear why he had such negative self-talk. We were now armed with the information and understanding about how he thinks, what his struggles are, and how we can try to support him.

It was an incredibly eye-opening and humbling moment as a parent. All those times we were frustrated and upset at his behaviour, all those times we thought he was being a spoilt only child, it was his neurodivergent brain that was unable to regulate his emotions, leading to a meltdown.

I walked out of that appointment vowing to do better and to be better, to work harder at understanding him so I could be the parent he needed. I knew how hard things had been for me. Then I thought, *hang on, he's the same as me! If my son has ADHD, then what do I have? I had/have all the same struggles he does.* So, armed with his diagnosis, I took myself off to an adult psychologist. Here is the list I took to him outlining my struggles.

ABOUT ME: KELLIE-ANNE GALLAGHER

- I'm extremely sensitive to facial expressions, voice and body movements
- Told I was a highly sensitive emotional empath.
- I am anxious and my husband is avoidant in relationship styles. If we fight and he doesn't sort it out with me right away, it sends me into a full-blown panic attack/meltdown.
- I've had many panic attacks.
- I can't have caffeine; it gives me anxiety and the shakes.
- Time – I'm constantly rushing. I only just make it on time. I'm constantly anxious about time.

- Spend hours scrolling on the phone at the end of the night or during the day to calm down.
- I'm an anxious, assertive, angry driver. I hate traffic and can't wait. I will take other route so that I don't have to sit and wait in traffic.
- I can't stand waiting in line at grocery stores. People standing too close to me makes me anxious.
- I hate clocks. I don't have one in my home. I don't like anything keeping the time.
- I never read instructions. I figure it out or put it together by working it out myself.
- I always have to say sorry and interrupt when I have something to say in a conversation. Otherwise, I find people just talk over the top of me.
- I can't stand people who talk at me and not to me. It frustrates me so much, to the point I feel physically sick and sometimes I'll either make up an excuse to leave or I'll just walk off.
- If I don't write an idea down in an email or text, I forget whatever it is I need to do.
- Can never find my phone.
- My thoughts are not linear. I have multiple tabs open in my brain all the time. I can jump from conversation to conversation. I don't always start at the start of the conversation. I have a roundabout way of explaining things and it drives my husband crazy.
- My handwriting changes. It's always messy. Sometimes I'll accidentally write letters the wrong way around or back to front. I do this with numbers as well. I make careless mistakes because I don't take the time to check things.
- But I can write neatly on a page without looking.
- I love to throw things out. I can't stand clutter.
- Too much mess makes me feel anxious and overwhelmed and I feel like I'm going to explode inside.
- I'm a high achiever/over-achiever.

- I can't handle chipped nail polish. If it happens, I obsess about it.
- I buy two pairs of the same shoes or clothes in multiple colours in the same style. I have many of the same things I just can't buy one of.
- I am a serial pimple-picker. I have done it for years. I've got scars on my face from it, and I will spend hours at it. Every single pore basically has to be squeezed. This happens when I'm really stressed.
- I binge-eat – especially chocolate.
- I crave cola. I had to quit it for about 10 years of my life because I drank so much of it.
- Holidays make me yo-yo happy-sad because of the family conflict that I've been through.
- I struggle with repeating thoughts, especially if in a conflict situation or if I feel unsafe, fearful thoughts about a situation that just happened continuously repeat and loop in my brain.
- I'm excellent at solving problems and making things fit. I'm a excellent multitasker. When motivated, I can get so much done. I've packed up an entire house with a one-and-a-half-year-old in one day.
- I get anxious if I don't exercise or move, I have to do this every day.
- I'm sensitive. I can't handle injustice, I can't handle liars. If I'm in an argument, I'm like a machine gun with the truth. I can't remember anything now, but then when I'm in a conflict or an argument with someone I can remember something that happened eight years ago.
- I cry easily. I am an empath – I feel like people's pain or illnesses are happening to me and so I don't watch the news.
- I think I have adrenal burnout.
- I get frightened very easily. I'm a very jumpy person.
- I can't watch anything gory, scary or violent.

- I struggle with intrusive thoughts, especially if I've been triggered or if I feel unsafe. I always think of the worst-case scenario or something happening, especially to my loved ones, worrying constantly about Junior makes me very conscious of safety, so I am constantly moving things so that he's safe.
- My brain obsesses over injustice, especially family conflict that we've had. I always think of the worst-case scenario, what the person is going to do next, so I can protect/save myself from being attacked. I'm constantly trying to arm myself for the next attack.
- I have negative self-thoughts. My default is always to pick on myself. I'm useless, worthless and I don't deserve to be here.
- I don't like to eat or drink the last of anything in a container. I'm always suspicious if something is off, and I throw a lot of things out.
- I struggled badly in school, especially with maths and music. I cannot read music. I learnt how to cheat, I learnt how to play music off by heart. I have no idea how to read music, but I still managed to achieve Bs to As in all subjects.
- Maths, I absolutely struggle with. Things just don't make sense to me, no matter how much someone explains them. I always thought I had a learning difficulty, but no one took me seriously, so I became very good at cheating in tests to get through, and then in high school I just didn't do maths as a subject because I struggled so badly.
- I always forget if the stove or the iron is off. I always have to check, and it's always off. Sometimes I have to drive back home just to check it, even though I am 90 per cent sure I turned it off.
- I obsessively lock my car doors. I must press the button at least three or four times to make sure that the door is locked.

- I'm a people pleaser. I hate saying no, In fact, I feel anxious saying no; I feel sick and overwhelmed. I don't feel comfortable choosing what I want.
- I hate making decisions, especially important major decisions. I leave all those up to my husband.
- At period time when my hormones are out of balance or if I'm having a miscarriage or if I'm pregnant, I struggle. I'm really tired. I get overwhelmed easily. I'm angry and more likely to have one of those meltdowns if there is a conflict between me and my husband.
- I suffer from avoidance. Some days I can sit all day in front of the computer and just struggle to get anything done, and then in the last hour before school pick-up I'll manage to cram a whole day's work in.
- I hate making phone calls. I hate taking phone calls. My phone gives me extreme anxiety.
- My emails give me anxiety.
- I hate doing things like booking a car service and then going there to pick my car up because that's out of my routine, so I just refuse to do it and then feel sick about not doing it.
- I do not like to go in cabs or Ubers.
- I do not know at all how to make small talk, as I'd rather not talk at all.
- I will avoid situations so that I don't have to be near anyone that I don't know without my husband being there.
- I intensely dislike bright lights, especially lights on during the day. I just will not have lights on in the house during the day.
- I get told by my husband all the time that I talk too loudly when I'm excited. I don't even know that I'm doing it.
- I'm super creative.
- I am literal, and I think others are literal, so it surprises be when people do the opposite of what they say.
- I have hyper focus I am excellent at problem-solving.

- I'm excellent at making things fit, like packing the car. It's like a game of Tetris for me and I always find the best way to do something.
- I cannot stand pressure.
- I dread stress or deadlines.
- My husband is an extremely driven a business owner, and he has many goals. He can handle lots of pressure and packs in as much as he can, and he still can thrive. I'm really struggling. I feel overwhelmed. I don't feel good enough. I can't handle it that I'm not the kind of person he is.
- I daydream.
- I cannot sit through a movie. I get bored I have to look at my phone.
- I'm rushing everywhere constantly. My son tells me to slow down when we are walking.
- I cook in a rush. My husband jokingly calls me a 'slapper' because I'm doing things so quickly. I can work in a 20 centimetre space and have a mess around me when I'm in the kitchen, and it just blows his mind.
- Sometimes I find it impossible to get out of bed, but I do anyway because I force myself… it feels like I'm walking through quicksand or mud.
- I'm extremely competitive. I believe this has helped mask my issues and have to do my best. In the gym I give 100 per cent in my workout. I'm all or nothing.
- I hate talking to strangers. I will avoid or pretend I don't see people I know to avoid talking to them. I won't answer calls, and take days to text back.
- I have severe social anxiety. I'm the kind of woman who is looking forward to a night out, and will cancel plans or won't go.
- As a child I hated talking to people. I would hide behind my parents. I could barely string a sentence together. I hated hugs from anyone other than my parents as it made me feel uncomfortable.

- I stuttered as a child. I sometimes do that now when I'm tripping over my words.
- I don't want to be without my husband or my son. I never want to leave them. I don't want to go anywhere without them.
- I have a habit of withdrawing from everyone, especially if I'm going through something difficult. I don't tell people because I don't want to be a burden.
- I can suffer from insomnia. I just cannot switch my brain off. I take melatonin to help me sleep.
- I had a very difficult childhood. I no longer have any contact with some close family members. When I fell pregnant with my son I instantly became protective of my child and didn't want him to go through what I went through.
- I have severe endometriosis. In 2017 I nearly lost my life to a post-operative infection. I had a laparoscopy to treat my endometriosis and got an infection and then spent nearly a month in hospital fighting for my life as my body was septic. I had subsequent surgery and a fallopian tube was removed. I had recurring miscarriages and lots of emotional and hormonal highs and lows, which I've really struggled with lately.
- My symptoms have become obvious now that I'm aware of what my son suffered with ADHD.
- I've researched and realised that I believe that I suffer from it myself.
- My childhood was full of conflict and I was in constant fight or flight mode.
- I think that a lot of things were missed because I was a good student in the sense that I got good grades, but the amount I struggled and how difficult it was for me went unnoticed.
- I was constantly in trouble for talking to friends at the wrong time or daydreaming.

- I developed an eating disorder as I never felt good enough. This is something I got over myself by practicing self-acceptance.
- I've had three strokes, heart surgery, Bell's palsy, breast augmentation which I immediately regretted and then had removed six years later due to implant illness.
- I believe the fact that I'm in flight or flight mode most of my life is because of the people I had to deal with. This is the reason my ADHD symptoms were masked so well. Now I'm doing a major work with a kinesiologist/psychologist and doing a lot of healing and personal growth, trying to calm down my nervous system.
- I'm trying to understand how my brain works to help myself be able to help my son better.
- I think I've had a nervous breakdown.
- As a kid I was told not to do things and I'd compulsively do the opposite, like I walked up and put my knee on the hot exhaust of a bike and burned myself. I knew it was stupid and shouldn't do it, but I did it because I was told not to.
- I am clumsy. I am always covered in bruises. Once I accidentally ripped off my toenail in a fluster while rushing somewhere.
- I was plagued by nightmares as a child.
- I never forget faces, but can't remember names. We have had two new apprentices in our business for the last four months and I can't remember the name of either of them.
- I get numbers and words jumbled, and write and say them the wrong way round a lot.
- I can't ever relax.
- Dogs panting stresses me out. If my dogs are panting, I can't be near them. It's illogical, but I can't stand it.
- I never understand or remember how I got somewhere.
- I'm constantly fidgeting.
- I impulse buy when I'm upset.

- I was extremely athletic. I would make district and sometimes regionals with no training in all kinds of athletics carnivals.
- I'm creative and love to paint.
- I was offered the opportunity to complete a Diploma in fashion design at the University of Queensland straight out of high school, something I always wanted to do, and declined. I'm too scared of change of routine.
- I listen to music and I hear every lyric. I can't ever listen to music to relax, because I listen to every word. If I need to relax to music, it has to be instrumental, otherwise I can't unwind. I can listen to the same song on repeat a hundred times and it doesn't bother me.
- I could eat the same meal for breakfast, lunch and dinner and it wouldn't bother me.
- I can see the same piece of rubbish on the floor but will walk over it a hundred times before I force myself to pick it up.
- My whole body is always tense, especially between my shoulders. They are always sore to touch.
- I can read a very thick book in a day.
- My hyperfocus is unmatched, and I get extremely irritated if interrupted.
- My son can be extremely demanding of attention and I struggle when I'm tired. I zone out at the end of the day. I need alone time when he's asleep to recover from overload.
- I will do anything for my son. My love and drive for him helps me force myself out of struggling to be a better person and parent for him. I've been to a counsellor, a psychologist, a kinesiologist and a hypnotist to be the best I can be and to break generational patterns and enable him to live his best life, loved and happy.
- I'm always stressed and overwhelmed. Sometimes mess in the house upsets me so much I feel like I will be physically sick or explode.

- Demands with work – all the emails, numbers and money, and things to remember. I always feel like I'm forgetting things. I dread work. I force myself to do things that feel physically impossible for me at times, with all the miscarriages the health issues and being plagued with intrusive thoughts, worrying about the next attack from family. I'm completely burned out. I possibly had a nervous breakdown or am about to have one.

* * *

I only got through about ten things on my list when the psychologist told me I have ADHD. In follow-up appointments and further discussions I was diagnosed with autism spectrum disorder, premenstrual dysphoric disorder (PMDD), post-traumatic stress disorder (PTSD) and dyscalculia, a learning disorder that affects the ability to understand number-based information.

I know that was a lot, but it's my story and so I am sharing it with you to help you feel less alone or lost at sea in your emotions, and to know that no matter what you go through, you can get through it. Knowledge is power. Understanding how you think and function is the power you need to thrive as a neurodivergent.

* * *

THIRTY-NINE YEARS IS a long time to live without understanding why you react the way you do. Why things affect you as they do, and why you are unable to function the same as everyone else. So now instead of telling myself I am useless or hopeless or stupid I say: you are a legend! Look how far you have come and how successful you are, in spite of all the difficulties you faced along the way. You never gave up. You never got bitter, you got better. You stepped up, showed up, put in the hard work, educated yourself, healed yourself and protected your child in the process. You didn't find excuses or play the victim. You found a way. And now I can say f**k you to everyone who treated me like crap or put me down. You didn't break me. I got better.

***

There are some crazy statistics that one girl to every three boys is diagnosed with ADHD. In adulthood, for every two males diagnosed, there is one woman diagnosed with ADHD. So there is a massive group of women who are being missed. It's not until our children are diagnosed that we realise that we may be too. Knowledge is power, so give yourself the kindness, empathy and patience you deserve.

My son was diagnosed at a younger age, but that doesn't mean he isn't going to face the same struggles and difficulties that I have.

Neurodivergent people have a unique way of operating, a unique way of thinking. There is nothing wrong with you. Remember that.

Most neurotypicals don't understand the difficulties we face living in a world where they want you to sit still, be quiet, follow the rules, not think outside the square. But I want you to be bold, and as loud and as creative as possible. I want you to live this life at the volume that you want to. I want you to think of it all, feel it all, do it all, and back yourself. No more trying to squash a square peg in a round hole. You be you.

Find your people, ones who respect and love that big, kind, deep heart of yours. Don't let others' inability to understand you hold you back. I don't want you to waste another day beating yourself up internally because you're not like everyone else. That's what's magical about you. Every single one of your neurodivergent traits makes you who you are. You are intuitive, empathetic, confident; a leader, bold, fearless, kind and loving. Stay that way forever. Whenever you feel lost or low, that's okay. It's part of the human experience and whenever you need it, my advice is here to guide you.

Each chapter covers a subject that is super-important to me and has little bits of wisdom and things that helped me. It's everything I wish I was told and had to learn the hard way. I hope it helps you.

HOW I UNDERSTAND ADHD

From my deep dive into my symptoms, this is what I have found so far. As more people are diagnosed every year, that equals awareness – and hopefully less stigma and more research.

- ADHD is a complex neurodevelopmental disorder which affects a person's ability to exert appropriate self-control.
- People with ADHD can have patterns of inattentive, impulsive, and sometimes hyperactive behaviour, together with difficulties in regulating their emotions.
- ADHD can have co-existing conditions that include autism spectrum disorder (ASD), anxiety, depression, learning disabilities, obsessive-compulsive disorder, sensory processing disorder, and oppositional defiant disorder, premenstrual dysphoric disorder and rejection sensitive dysphoria.
- Everyone presents slightly different ADHD symptoms.

There are many positive attributes to ADHD that don't get spoken about enough. For example, someone with ADHD can be extremely empathetic, energetic, very spontaneous, super creative, intuitive and imaginative. They can hyperfocus on interests, are adventurous, enthusiastic and make great leaders in group situations.

While ADHD is a neurobiological developmental disorder – no one knows exactly what causes it.

WHAT I UNDERSTAND PMDD TO BE

PMDD is a condition that causes severe emotional and psychological distress in the lead-up to your period, brought on by the hormonal changes at that time. PMDD is more than bad premenstrual syndrome (PMS). It causes extreme highs and low lows, anger and an inability to deal with things in day-to-day life that wouldn't normally upset you. Feelings of depression, hopelessness, worthlessness or extreme guilt. You can feel tense and anxious, overwhelmed and out of control – sometimes all at once. These symptoms can last a week or two, or even longer in some cases. It has been the cause of relationships falling apart, because partners find it hard to understand the extreme changes in the sufferer's personality and moods. If you feel like this and can relate, please see your doctor as soon as possible. There is no need to suffer any longer.

WHAT I UNDERSTAND RSD TO BE

Rejection sensitivity disorder, or RSD, is when a person experiences severe emotional pain due to a failure or feeling rejected. A small misunderstanding can lead you to fear that people don't like you. It is linked to ADHD, and the difficulty in regulating your emotions means your brain can't regulate rejection-related emotions and behaviours, making everything feel far more intense. It can lead to relationship breakdowns and a fear of trying new things due to the intense fear of rejection.

* * *

IF YOU FIND anything in this book relatable, I urge you to take control of your life and your mental health. See your general practitioner; investigate your symptoms. Knowledge equals power, and understanding how you think gives you the power you need to heal and live the best life you deserve.

THE UPSIDE OF BEING
NEURODIVERGENT

*I*f you are neurodivergent – or think you may be – you'll understand that its positive traits aren't spoken about enough. Outdated belief systems focus on the negatives, so when you are diagnosed, it's hard to believe that there's anything good about being neurodivergent.

I want that to change that. If you are neurodivergent, you will possess some incredible and unique gifts.

If you have ADHD, you will have a very vivid imagination and excel at tasks that require creativity, such as drawing or storytelling, and are often excellent at solving problems. Our high energy and enthusiasm can be channelled into things we love. Our passion for our special interests makes us interesting and fun to be around. Hello hyperfocus! We possess a natural curiosity to learn about our special interests, and a desire to learn new things.

Neurodivergents can be very detail-oriented, especially if you have OCD. You have strong attention to detail, and you may also have a strong sense of responsibility and a desire to get things 'right'. This can make you reliable and conscientious. You will also have an extreme sense of empathy, sensitivity and compassion. This makes you highly attuned to the feelings of people around you.

Autism means you are direct, honest, and have a strong sense of justice. There is no fluff to your conversation, it's to the point and often very factual. Your love for the truth and for justice makes you loyal and trustworthy.

When managing multiple conditions, your problem-solving skills will become exceptional. You have no choice, it will give you resilience and creative problem-solving abilities. You will learn to be adaptive and find innovative ways to manage your challenges, which will benefit all areas of your life.

You develop perseverance and the ability to keep going despite the difficulties you may face with being neurodivergent in a neurotypical world.

* * *

BEING NEURODIVERGENT IS A GIFT. It can make you strong and capable of handling adversity. You will also develop coping strategies. Managing your different conditions can lead to a strong desire for self-improvement and a deeper understanding of oneself. Use this to motivate yourself to make a positive impact on the world. Please do not think that being neurodivergent is a negative thing – it is a positive thing. Be the alchemist and turn the negatives into positives, embracing both love and light.

I believe that being neurodivergent with enhanced sensory abilities in your own unique way means you will have your own unique spiritual gifts, and I urge you to explore these. Here are some of the spiritual gifts I have found with my neurodivergence.

1. HEIGHTENED SENSORY AWARENESS AND MINDFULNESS

If you are on the autism spectrum or have sensory processing differences, you can often have heightened sensory awareness. This heightened sensitivity can mean you experience deep mindfulness and presence, as you are naturally more attuned to your surroundings.

This can lead to profound spiritual experiences, such as feeling deeply connected to nature, music or other sensory-rich environments.

2. EXPERIENCE ALTERED STATES OF CONSCIOUSNESS

With some neurodivergent conditions, like ADHD and autism, you can sometimes experience moments that are like altered states of consciousness. For example, when you are experiencing hyperfocus it can feel like you are in a deep meditative state, where time seems to stand still, and there is an intense feeling of being in the present moment. Altered states develop spiritual insight and a sense of oneness with the universe.

3. YOU HAVE OUT OF THE BOX THINKING

If you are neurodivergent, you often think in a non-linear, abstract way, which can align with spiritual or alternative thinking. The ability to think beyond conventional, linear logic allows for a deep exploration of spiritual concepts, such as the meaning of existence, interconnectedness, or the divine and your soul's true purpose.

You may feel more attuned to spirituality or have a natural affinity for mystical practices and philosophies. Because neurodivergents don't always conform to traditional ways of thinking or learning, they can bring fresh, unconventional ideas that challenge the status quo and drive progress.

4. DEEP EMPATHY AND COMPASSION

Being neurodivergent means you will experience deep feelings of empathy, especially those with autism or on the spectrum. Your compassion and deep sense of connection to other people or animals makes you hyperaware of our interconnectedness or oneness with the universe and nature.

A deep sense of empathy leads to care and compassion for other beings and for the natural world. You care deeply for those you love, and show great kindness and a desire for unity.

5. UNIQUE SPIRITUAL INSIGHTS AND REVELATIONS

Neurodivergent people can experience unique spiritual insights and revelations due to our different ways of processing information and perceiving the world. We can have a fresh perspective on spirituality, religion or metaphysical concepts, often challenging conventional beliefs and offering new understandings of spiritual truths.

6. A STRONG SENSE OF BEING 'DIFFERENT' OR 'OTHER'

The feeling of being different can be through having enhanced memory and recall. Those with autism or certain types of learning differences may have strong memory skills, particularly in areas like visual recall. Neurodivergents can be excellent at recognising patterns and noticing details that others might overlook. I never forget a face and I can pack anything efficiently and quickly. It takes no effort for me, but for others these things could take hours.

This skill can be incredibly valuable in fields such as mathematics, science and coding, and more so if you have heightened sensory awareness. Your sensitivity can enhance experiences and contribute to talents in areas like music, art or anything creative, with talents that seem otherworldly. My son, for example, can pick up a guitar and play a tune he has only heard once, and play it instantly without music to read. He intuitively knows where the notes are and can play by ear.

Diagnosed or undiagnosed, you will have a profound sense of being different from the norm, which leads to a deep longing for meaning and purpose. This quest for understanding one's place in the world and the universe can lead to a spiritual journey, often involving deep personal reflection, exploration of spiritual practices, and a quest for personal and collective meaning. My desire to write this book came from that.

7. INCREASED SENSITIVITY TO ENERGY

Being neurodivergent means I have an increased sensitivity to the energy around me, whether it be emotional or a general sense of spiritual or environmental energy. I instinctively know when something feels 'off' and I have a deep sense of knowing when something is right. My heightened sensitivity has made me more attuned to spiritual experiences, such as feeling a strong connection with nature and animals and sensing the energy of places.

8. A DEEP FEELING OF CONNECTION TO NATURE AND THE UNIVERSE

If you are neurodivergent, you can feel a profound connection to nature and the cosmos. I definitely do. I have a natural sense of wonder and desire to find out my purpose and the meaning to life.

9. INTUITIVE UNDERSTANDING AND INNER KNOWING

Being neurodivergent means I often rely on intuition and inner knowing; this is a powerful spiritual tool. I learnt to use this intuitive sense to guide me in my spiritual practices, decision-making, and understanding of myself. After years of unlearning rigid religious beliefs, I have learnt to tap into my own inner guidance system that all the answers I need are within me. It has been a fun journey of self-discovery.

10. CHALLENGE AND GROWTH AS SPIRITUAL PRACTICE

The challenges that we often come with being neurodivergent, such as navigating a world that isn't always accommodating, has been a part of my spiritual journey. Challenges neurodivergents face have forced me on a trajectory of personal growth. I've developed resilience and a deeper understanding of myself and my spiritual path. For many neurodivergent people, our unique perspectives and experiences are a form of spiritual practice, embracing differences as a sacred part of who we are. It's our gift.

* * *

THE SPIRITUAL CONNECTIONS that come with experiencing neurodivergence are deeply personal and diverse. You will have a wide range of experiences and perceptions unique to you. So being neurodivergent has many positive attributes. I am so grateful for my unique attributes, the unique way I experience life. I am finally embracing who I am and am using my gifts instead of trying to hide or ignore them. This has enriched my life and it is my hope that you embrace yours and see neurodivergence as an incredible gift and an opportunity experience life in a deeper way.

THE WORDS YOU SPEAK

*L*et's start with the words you speak. They are the creation of your life, the verbal spells you weave every day that send you on a positive or negative trajectory.

I became aware of the words you speak and their importance when my hit health rock bottom. I almost died from a post-operative infection. The doctor prepared my husband for the likelihood that I wasn't going to make it (unbeknown to me). While I was in hospital and desperate to get better, I Googled quotes by Tony Robbins. I read how important words are and I said to the universe, 'this isn't how my story ends, I will not die this way. I fought too hard and too long to have my son to leave him after two-and-a-half years. I will get better; I will leave this hospital. Show me how to heal myself so I will never be this sick again. Let me be the mother I always wanted to be to my son. Please heal me. Thank you, thank you, thank you.' I repeated the mantra, 'thank you for my healing' over and over again, never wavering in my faith no matter how sick I was and how hopeless the situation seemed. By my willpower and statements to the universe I walked out of that hospital.

Lucas means 'bringer of light'. You are the light of my life!

FOR YOU, LOVE ME

"Words are energy and cast spells — that's why it's called spelling." - Bruce Lee

25

THE WORDS you speak build the house you live in.

What does that mean? What you say is so powerful in shaping your life. What you say out loud and your internal dialogue.

When you speak it sends out a vibration. Vibration equals energy, positive or negative, so be aware of what you say.

Are you only speaking negatively? If so, this will lower your vibration so when you catch yourself talking negatively – this includes swearing (I have the worst potty mouth and it's something I'm working on) – turn it around and say something positive, internally if that feels more comfortable for you.

You are human, and if you are neurodivergent, your brain is like a racing car going at a hundred miles per hour, or like a computer with several tabs open. You aren't always going to speak perfectly, but try to make a conscious effort to speak positively and don't forget to let others speak.

Yes, we get super enthusiastic when there is a topic we relate to or that interests us, so try not to dominate conversations in your enthusiasm. Listen to hear, not to talk. You can unintentionally annoy or push others away by 'taking over a conversation' in a bid to relate by sharing our shared experiences. Conversing is like walking a tightrope to neurodivergents; we are either flat out or not at all and if you have verbal diarrhoea, oversharing will leave you feeling anxious and depleted, worrying if you said to much. So, try to relax, take a breath and wait for your turn to share.

You know the saying: If the words you spoke appeared on your skin, would you still be beautiful?

BECOME AWARE OF YOUR SELF-TALK

This is a big one for neurodivergents. Our internal dialogue can be so negative. Feeling like you're different and defective because this world is not programmed to suit our way of thinking can leave you with a lot of negative self-talk. Remember, there is nothing wrong with you. You are perfect the way you are. Don't take out the frustrations of the difficulties functioning as a neurodivergent on yourself. You didn't choose to be neurodivergent; it is who you are and who you are is perfect.

So, in those moments of negativity remember: speak words of gratitude for anything. For example, give thanks for the gift of life the second you wake up. Say 'thank you' and feel the gratitude in your body. This sets the direction of your day. It instantly changes your vibe

Your body is incredible. Its sole purpose is to keep you alive. Every day it does its best for you.

When you look in the mirror, say 'thank you'. Remember that words are vibration and send yourself love and kindness. Imagine what you would say to your younger self. You wouldn't be mean and make harsh judgements, so treat yourself with all the kindness and love you deserve.

How you respect yourself sets the benchmark for how others respect you.

KELLIE-ANNE GALLAGHER

— 'THE WORDS YOU SPEAK ARE POWERFUL. ESPECIALLY THE WORDS YOU SPEAK TO YOURSELF.' — ROBIN S. SHARMA

ENERGY, INTUITION AND VIBRATION

Remember: energy doesn't lie!

From my experience as a neurodivergent, you notice and feel so much more than other people. You are aware of energies, so I want you to protect your energy and make sure you don't give everyone access to it. It will only drain you and leave you depleted.

I was diagnosed with ADHD and autism, PMDD and dyscalculia at 39, and then my life suddenly made sense. I have always been in tune with and hypersensitive to others' emotions and energies, often before they are themselves aware of what they are feeling. It's a spiritual gift. And I was often told that I over-think, I'm paranoid, blah blah blah... Guess what, I wasn't wrong. I can predict a person's behaviour; I can tell if they are lying and if they are hiding something, or if they are sad. If you are neurodivergent, there's a very high chance you can too. Listen to your intuition. If there is one important lesson I want you to learn, it's don't let anyone convince you that what you are feeling isn't true or real.

You have an in-built warning system called your intuition. Listen to it. Your body picks up on vibrations – good or bad – before your mind does. It is your inner guidance system.

There have been many times I've listened to my intuition. I have never regretted a decision I made by doing so.

If someone asks you to go somewhere or to do something and it doesn't feel right, don't ignore the feeling. Alternatively, if you are offered a promotion or the chance to do something and you feel instant excitement and joy, say yes, do it! The ADHD brain can be impulsive and chase the dopamine hit. I want you to always trust your gut instinct. It never lies.

If you get full body tingles or shivers, it's your soul recognising the truth.

FOR YOU, LOVE ME

'Trust your intuition, it is the best friend you will ever have.'— Judith Orloff

IF YOU MEET someone and their vibe is off, trust your intuition, or if you meet someone and it's an instant, obsessive attraction, they aren't for you. People who are for you bring you peace. Always remember that.

GOOD VIBES ONLY

The saying 'your vibe attracts your tribe' is so true. If you speak negativity, gossip, or words of hate, that's the energy of the people, places and situations you will attract. Speak words of peace, joy, love, and positivity and that's the energy of the people, places and opportunities you will attract.

In life, if you don't like the situation you are in, observe and change where needed.

> *Love is the highest vibration.*
> *God is love. Speak words of love.*

WHEN FACED WITH DIFFICULT SITUATIONS, create a simple, positive mantra to get you through. For example, when you're doing something that scares you, repeat, 'I am alright, I am okay'. Take a deep breath and repeat; it will calm you and help you through.

When in doubt, when you feel lost, go to where the love is. By doing what you love, saying what you love and being with those who you love.

FOR YOU, LOVE ME

Have the courage to follow your heart and intuition.
— Steve Jobs

PURPOSE

I believe our purpose as humans is to love, find connections, experience joy and peace, and to overcome negativity by choosing love.

As you get older and you don't just live for the moment, as most of us did when we were young, you will start to question your purpose. Us neurodivergent people can become excited and fixated on one thing and be completely uninterested the next day.

Imposter syndrome and self-doubt can steal your dreams, so write down what you want. Look at your life: does it reflect this? If not, change it. This can help you find your direction.

There is no rush to find your purpose. Don't put pressure on yourself and lose the joy in self-discovery. It will come to you naturally when it is meant to.

Whenever you feel lost, ask yourself, what do I love? What brings me joy? Go where your heart desires. Don't spend your life living to make someone else happy.

FOR YOU, LOVE ME

— *'WHY FIT IN WHEN YOU WERE BORN TO STAND OUT?'*
— *DR SEUSS*

We had our son so we could shower him with love and watch him grow, not to mould him and stop him from living his life to the fullest.

This is your life. Live it to the fullest. Spread your wings and go in whatever direction your heart takes you.

We are all born with the same choices: who do we want to be and how do we want to act? What legacy and impressions do we want to leave on the world when we pass?

FOR YOU, LOVE ME

— *'YOUR PURPOSE IN LIFE IS TO FIND YOUR PURPOSE
AND GIVE YOUR WHOLE HEART AND SOUL TO IT.'* —
BUDDHA

If you are unsure what your purpose is, then give back. Help others at home, at work, with friends and family. The act of giving from a place of love with no expectation of receiving anything in return is a love-inspired action that in turn sets in motion positive action. One step made with love is a step in right direction to find your purpose.

The amount of success you attract is determined by the person you become. It's the law of attraction.

ADOPT AN ATTITUDE OF GRATITUDE

Seek others whose success or career reflects your own dreams and desires, and use this as a guide for your own goals and growth to achieve your dreams.

I believe that part of everyone's purpose here on Earth is to express gratitude, big or small, for every wonderful thing in their life. To be present in every moment is a chance for you to raise your vibration, choose love and express gratitude.

If you find yourself in a fork in the road, I believe it's an opportunity for a reset.

Now we aren't perfect and it's not always going to be easy, but the more you do it, the easier it is, until it becomes your default action or second nature to you.

Go with the flow. Write down your heart's desires, your life goals, what you want to have achieved by the time you are eighty years old. Then set about achieving these goals and let the natural flow of manifestation get you what you want – or something even better.

Once you find your purpose, your hopes, dreams and goals, be careful who you tell. Some people want to see you do well, but just not better than them, so keep those precious heart's desires close so no one can discourage you with their limited or negative thinking.

In the process of finding your purpose, don't become your own roadblock through limitation and lack of action. Allow yourself to receive gifts, compliments and help. Don't stop the flow of love others are trying to send your way.

KELLIE-ANNE GALLAGHER

What you are thinking now is creating your future life. —
Rhonda Byrne

FOLLOWING your heart and doing what you love raises the vibration and adds to the positive energy in this world, which is something that it desperately needs.

You must act on your desires. Don't make the mistake of waiting for them to fall in your lap. Want to be a CEO? Get off your ass and work at it: get up early, be the last employee home, prove yourself worthy. Want your own business? Then educate yourself. Want to be a professional athlete or an artist? Then train, be consistent, be confident, take the chances. Back yourself in whatever it may be that you want. You can and will achieve your dreams!

FEAR OF REJECTION

Rejection sensitivity disorder can inhibit you from achieving your dreams. Don't let fear rob you of what you want. Remember, fear is a lack of love, a lack of trust and faith that the universe has your back. Back yourself. Bet on yourself. Get grounded and confident in your abilities and what you have to offer. Ignore that negative voice inside your head telling you can't. You can!

You will either find a way or an excuse.
You get to choose...

OUR PURPOSE IS TO CREATE. Creation comes in all forms. It is a form of expression that is good for the soul. Everyone's idea of creating is different, if you love art, then paint; if you love music, then play. Even the way you present yourself is a form of self-expression and creation.

Your life is your masterpiece, and you are the artist!

KELLIE-ANNE GALLAGHER

Do everything with love and joy in your heart and release the expectation of what creation 'should' look like. Don't restrict yourself by chasing perfection. What is perfection anyway? Just create from the heart. We are also here to learn …

If you are not willing to learn, no one can help you. If you are determined to learn, no one can stop you.

FOR YOU, LOVE ME

'Everybody is a genius. But if you judge a fish by its ability to climb a tree, it will live its whole life believing that it is stupid.'
— Albert Einstein

LEARNING

*L*earning is one of the fun parts of the human experience, but can be a tough one for neurodivergents. We are wired differently. To be honest, I love the way I'm wired. I've finally got to a place where I don't give a shit that I am quirky, creative, out there and different. I love how I am and I hope it doesn't take you as long to accept yourself as it did me.

When it comes to learning, keep an open mind. I feel that anyone who has an extreme view for one thing or an extreme belief system is missing the point.

When we are born, we don't have all the answers; we have to learn every day. We never stop learning. You are growing and expanding your consciousness. Don't become stale – constantly evolve.

That's why we gave our son the middle name of Ocean, wonderful, fierce, ever-changing and uncontrollable.

You won't be the same person in five years' time, and that's okay. Go with the flow, like the ever-changing ocean.

* * *

HEARING this was one of the turning points in my life:

If you aren't prepared to change, you will never get ahead in life.

It spoke to my soul.

I thought, *what do I have to change to get ahead in life?* I turned inwards and thought, *what do I need to change about myself? What is keeping me stuck in a place where I am not happy?* And my personal growth journey began.

I also looked around at others who were unhappy. They had victim attitudes. It was everyone else's fault but theirs: why they hated their job, their partner and their life. They never changed or did anything about their situation. I didn't want that to be me.

KELLIE-ANNE GALLAGHER

— *'NOBODY WITH A VICTIM MENTALITY WILL GET ANYWHERE EVER. THEY WILL NEVER SUCCEED.' — JON LOVITZ*

No judgement. Everybody is on their own journey of self-discovery. I just knew *I* had to change.

I also asked myself, *who do I want to be and what kind of person are you?* I started to look for celebrities or motivational speakers who reflected the kind of person I wanted to become. I looked at the parts of my personality I need to work on to reflect their mindset and start to learn how to be the best person I can be.

Look for situations, relationships and things that keep repeating in your life. See where the patterns are.

Are you allowing certain kinds of people or situations to happen?

If they don't make you happy or don't align with your values, then change them.

Remove yourself from the situation. Remove yourself from their company. It's as simple as that.

If you see someone struggling, it is *their* own growth point. You don't need to 'fix' everyone. Focus on learning how to fix yourself. I learnt this the hard way!

STRUGGLE IS *YOUR* GROWTH POINT

Don't be an over-giver, expecting thanks for something takers never asked for. You are overcompensating for something. Stop, work out what that is, and help yourself first.

By all means ask if others need help, but do it within reason without expecting thanks in return. If it's done with love, gratitude from others is nice, but not needed.

Learn that some people sit in their struggles because they have something to gain from it, such as attention, self-sabotage or drama, because they thrive off the addictive energy or pain it brings. Some people find comfort in pain; it's all they are used to and you will never change that, unless they want you to. Sometimes people like to wallow in their own problems they create. Let them be.

FOCUS ON YOURSELF

To learn about yourself, journal. Write down your heart's desires, your goals and your plans, who you want to be. Set about learning how to become that person. And use your intuition as your guide.

I believe having an open mind that is uninhibited by rigid belief systems is the key to true happiness and the route to personal growth.

Don't be afraid of the lessons you have to learn in this lifetime. You have all the love and power inside yourself to get through anything. Go through life with love and excitement for the next adventure or possibility. Don't fear and avoid living because you are scared of what could happen. That is not living; that's existing. Live this life to the fullest. Do it with love and it will be a life well lived.

Do your best in school, but if its rigid structure isn't your thing, don't beat yourself up about it. There are many diagnosed and undiagnosed neurodivergent people that struggled at school and found their feet after they finished. They are some of the world's most successful athletes and businesspeople.

RELIGION, SPIRITUALITY AND GUILT

Religion has many beautiful messages, but while it may work for some, it has never sat right with me. I question why, if God is so loving, kind and forgiving, would he then damn someone to eternal hell? I don't agree at all. This is where guilt is used to control.

This is why we are letting our son find his own truths.

Any belief system governed by fear and guilt is ultimately just trying to control you.

The truth doesn't mind being questioned.

Therefore, restricting belief systems leave little room for personal growth because you're governed by fear. Remember, fear is a lack of love.

If you are relying on a rigid belief system to dictate your goals, dreams and your directions, that is manipulation and control.

Know that guilt is so destructive. Never let anyone guilt you for any reason to do anything you don't want to do. *Never.*

KELLIE-ANNE GALLAGHER

— 'RELIGION IS NEVER THE PROBLEM; IT'S THE PEOPLE
WHO USE IT TO GAIN POWER.' — JULIAN CASABLANCAS

IF THERE IS one thing I hope I pass on to you, it's to make decisions because *you want to.* Then, no matter the consequences of your decisions, you can live with the outcome because it was your choice, not anyone else's. (My husband told me this little pearl of wisdom.)

Because neurodivergents don't always fit the norm and we can feel guilty or not good enough, this kind of inner dialogue can make you susceptible to manipulation, guilt or staying somewhere or with someone longer than you should.

There is nothing wrong with you! Be proud of who you are and don't let anyone guilt you into anything.

Guilt is a blackness on the purity of your life. It is constricting and soul sucking.

The second you feel guilty, say no! No one, if they ever *truly* loved you or cared for you, would use guilt to manipulate you.

That is why I encourage you to discover your spirituality on your own. Your spirituality is so important. Find spiritual practices that align with your values. *This life is your life.* Take control. Follow your heart, find your truth. Believe in what resonates with your soul.

Pray, burn sage, do yoga, read books, educate yourself. Do whatever feels true to you.

The world is yours to discover.

KELLIE-ANNE GALLAGHER

— 'THE SPIRITUAL JOURNEY IS THE UNLEARNING OF
FEAR AND THE ACCEPTANCE OF LOVE.' — MARIANNE
WILLIAMSON

PAST LIVES, SPIRIT GUIDES AND ANGELS

*T*here is so much more to life than birth, work, death, and that's it.

As I mentioned, keep an open mind. The world is your oyster, don't let fear or outdated religious concepts dictate your decisions or beliefs.

A big part of my life's journey has been to unlearn restricting, rigid belief systems. That is my biggest motivator to raise my son free to find his own truths. Neurodiverse people can be extremely intuitive. We are more sensitive to light, sound, touch and smell – basically, to the world around us. We pick up on energies and intentions that often go unnoticed by others. I feel that getting in touch with your spirituality and your intuitive side helps in the healing process and your acceptance of your unique gifts.

There are many ways in which you can be guided; seek help and protection in your learning journey.

If you feel that there is a fear or a pattern of behaviour that you can't shake, then I encourage you to stop and go on your own journey of past life discovery, to heal.

Sometimes the past holds all the answers we need.

Western society treats past lives as taboo, but it is completely normal in Eastern society.

Sometimes past lives can hold the key to toxic patterns, emotions and situations that are happening in this life. You need to heal from the past to be able to move on in the present.

Seek out certified Quantum Healing Hypnosis Technique past life regressionists and hypnotists, or find guided meditations, as I did, to regress to a past life, heal what needs to be healed, and move on.

There are way too many psychic mediums with proven success in contacting spirits and those who have passed on the 'other side' for their abilities not to be real. These topics are no longer taboo.

Find a psychic that speaks to your intuition. Not everyone suits everybody, so find your person and seek messages and guidance from the other side if you would like to venture down that road. It's not for everybody, and I understand that. But some of my most profound learning has come from the guidance from the 'other side'.

As I have said previously, trust your intuition; you will know when something sounds true to you. There is free will and nothing is set in stone. Every day you wake up and make your *own choices*.

Don't become reliant on anybody. I want you to learn to look inside yourself for answers, but there is help when you need it.

Ask the universe for a sign when making a decision you are unsure of.

Make your sign personal to you and say, 'If this is meant to be let me see my sign'.

We all have guardian angels who watch over us and guide us.

Trust that everything that happens is meant to be.

Everything that happens is a lesson or a blessing, and you are divinely guided and protected.

You are never alone, you are truly loved and guided along the way.

Ask your guides for help when it is needed. There are many books on the subject of angels and the divine help they offer. I personally believe in them, and if there is help on offer, I will gladly receive it. All you need to do is ask.

Always treat people with kindness and respect. Even if their belief system is different, there is beauty in all of it.

A lot of people walk around thinking that their unkind thoughts or actions can go unnoticed or without consequence. But a thought is a vibration and vibration is energy. Once created, energy can't be destroyed. Therefore, a negative action won't go unnoticed or without consequence. It's called the law of karma.

Know that what is done in darkness always comes to light. You can't hide dark intentions.

Choose the light, choose love, and leave others to learn their lessons in their own way. But don't judge people too harshly. We don't know everyone's journey, or their struggle and what they have been through.

Just protect yourself and your energy. Don't set about trying to fix everyone. People need to learn how to heal themselves. Remember, we are all here to heal and to learn and to do better, so if you lead with love, you can't, go wrong.

God is love.
You are love.
God is within you.
We are divine beings having a human experience.

KELLIE-ANNE GALLAGHER

— *"TRUE HEALING WILL ALWAYS BEGIN WITH YOUR THOUGHTS. MASTER YOUR THOUGHTS AND YOU WILL MASTER YOUR LIFE.' — APRIL PEERLESS*

HEALING MIND, BODY AND SOUL

On your journey of self-discovery, you will find there are parts of you that need to heal.

Everyone will need to heal from their childhood, including you.

I am constantly apologising to my son and my husband and owning my behaviour. I do the best I can. I love them and they motivate me to heal, be a cycle-breaker; to be better and do better.

Even if your childhood was 'perfect', no one escapes without something we need to heal.

BE A CYCLE-BREAKER

When you become a parent, if that's what you decide to do, whatever you haven't dealt with from your past you will pass on to your kids. It's unavoidable, and children are your mirror.

When you are healing, be kind to yourself.

Learn what you need to do to heal yourself. There is power in that. Find out what you need to do on your healing journey. Don't rely on others. Take control.

If you are undiagnosed or have been undiagnosed for a long time, there are a lot of traumas that can come with a missed diagnosis. Years of masking, years of overcompensation. Statistics show that a boy with ADHD will hear 20,000 more negative statements in seven short years of life than a neurotypical child (keep in mind most neurodiversity studies are based on boys, not girls). That's a lot you will need to unpack and heal from.

If you need therapy or someone to talk to, then bravely show up for yourself. If you need medication for a time, then speak to your GP to get the help you need. Don't let fear rob you of your healing.

Healing is like an onion, with many layers. Take one step/layer at a time.

If you have been dealing with a toxic or stressful situation for a long time, it takes a toll on your health. You can't heal while you are hurting.

I want you to remember that if you are in a stressful or toxic situation and there is no chance of you making it better, remove yourself. Not only will you have to heal your mind, you will also have to heal your body

Your body warns you; it shows you the things that you need to work on. Its warnings come by way of ill-health or discomfort. For example, if you are suffering from constant stomach upsets, it could mean you're in a situation that is not right for you, and you haven't processed the emotions.

One of the major things that I had to heal and break the cycle of was my lack of self-acceptance, my willingness to accept others' judgements of me and then punish myself for my perceived shortcomings.

I developed an eating disorder at the age of 18. Looking back, I wish I could hug my younger self. Tell 18-year-old me that my self-loathing, anxiety and frustration was because I was an undiagnosed autistic ADHD.

I had gone my whole life hearing I was not good enough and I should apply myself more. The constant the negative feedback wounded me deeply, as no one knew just how hard I was trying.

I finished school, moved out of home and faced the world with absolute trepidation and fear. How was I supposed to function and find a career when I could hardly speak to anybody, or look someone in the eye?

I would tell the younger me I wasn't stupid, I wasn't ugly, I wasn't a failure. Who cares what others think of your quirkiness? It's a reflection on them, not you, and you will meet your people. Be unafraid to be yourself and don't try to keep yourself small to 'fit in'. You will be okay, there is nothing wrong with you. Don't be so scared of the unknown; be as kind to yourself as you would be to five-year-old you. Have your own back, believe in yourself and everything will be okay as you have the ability to get through anything.

I was a young woman who had been overlooked in the school system because of my excellent ability to overcome and hide my shortcomings. I found a job in retail, and having to meet daily targets quickly got me to mask and overcome how uncomfortable I was interacting with strangers. While it was good in one way, it was eating me away inside. I just existed. Until one day I got down on my knees and I prayed: please send me my person, please send me the love of my life. Surely I am not meant to be this miserable for the rest of my life?

Two weeks later I met my person, my husband. The love of my life. I went from existing to living. My life is incredible; my healing is possible because that man is my safe place. He gave me unconditional love, something I had never experienced before, and the opportunity to find myself.

Over the last 20 years we have done some incredible personal growth together. We are polar opposites in every way and that presents its own challenges, but our love helps us overcome the differences and grow together, not apart.

If you have struggled like I have, I hope you meet your person. I hope you have your safe place to unmask and be yourself. I hope you find someone who values and accepts you for who you are. Don't stop until you do, because this life is incredible when you meet that soul who lifts you up shows you that you have wings and gives you the freedom to fly. The sky is the limit.

FOR YOU, LOVE ME

— 'HAPPILY EVER AFTER IS NOT A FAIRYTALE, IT'S A CHOICE.' – FAWN WEAVER

RELATIONSHIPS

Relationships are where your greatest blessings and lessons are hidden.

Now, I'm no expert, but I've narrowed people down into three categories: narcissists, empaths, and everyone else.

The quality of your relationship with yourself will be reflected in the quality of the relationships you have with other people.

What I mean by this is if you have a healthy self-love, a healthy understanding of what is right and wrong and what you will and won't accept (in other words, boundaries), then you're more than likely to be surrounded by like-minded, high-vibe, kind people.

But toxic people show up in your life to show you where you need to heal and to show you how to stand up for yourself.

I've met a few narcissists in my time, and they forced me to see the deepest parts of me that needed healing, turn a negative into a positive. Be an alchemist.

Remember: not everyone is going to like you, and that's okay.

Disagreements in relationships happen to help you see how you handle conflict. Dealing with difficult people teaches you to have your own back, not look to everyone else to save you.

The same situations and conflicts will keep arising with the same people (or different people) until you have learnt the lesson. So set boundaries for behaviour, for what you will and won't accept.

You have the right to choose in this life; you are not a victim. If you are unhappy, change your situation, look at what you need to change in yourself. Are you allowing toxic behaviour, or are you being toxic?

Have a look at *all* your relationships, who is toxic and who makes you feel safe, happy and loved when you are with them.

Your friend groups will grow and evolve as you change and that's okay. Don't feel the need to hold on tightly to anyone in your life. People will come and go to match your energy.

Remember, neurodivergents suffer from rejection sensitivity. Always try to give yourself and others grace, and really analyse whether you are being rejected or if your neurodivergence is making you feel that way. Your intuition will be your guide when you are unsure.

Rejection is protection, so if relationships drift apart there is a very good reason for it. It may be a reason you can't see yet, so don't hold on too tightly to anything that needs to be let go of and what is truly meant for you will find you.

Another important lesson is don't let the family that you came from ruin the family that you create.

KELLIE-ANNE GALLAGHER

— 'THE BOND THAT LINKS YOUR TRUE FAMILY IS NOT ONE OF BLOOD, BUT OF RESPECT AND JOY IN EACH OTHER'S LIFE.' – RICHARD BACH

IT IS NOT your responsibility to get someone to treat you better, and it is not your responsibility to accept somebody's toxic behaviour, no matter who they are.

So, while you may love them, you do not have to have them in your life. You can quietly, calmly and lovingly make peace inside yourself and cut the energetic cord to that person and remove them from your life.

It's not your job to try and heal someone else, or to teach them how to respect your boundaries. Your job is to notice who honours them and who doesn't, and allow them in your circle accordingly.

Allow every situation, disagreement and conflict to be what it is. Don't try to be the fixer. Be polite. Act with love and respect, but keep those boundaries firmly in place.

KELLIE-ANNE GALLAGHER

— *'LETTING GO MEANS TO COME TO THE REALIZATION THAT SOME PEOPLE ARE A PART OF YOUR HISTORY, BUT NOT A PART OF YOUR DESTINY.' – STEVE MARABOLI*

SOME PEOPLE ARE ON A TOXIC, destructive path, and they don't care who they drag down with them. That is unfair. They will have to work out their own karma, but don't get caught up trying to stop or fix the lesson someone else needs to learn.

Sometimes it's easier to just quietly exit stage left without expecting an apology. Trust your instincts. Analyse their pattern of behaviour; it's a pretty good indication of how they will treat you. Some people who genuinely love you and care for you will stop, say sorry the moment you tell them, and change. That is love.

Others, if you tell them they are hurting you, may just open a whole can of worms that should have stayed shut and cause far more upset and hurt in the process. These people are toxic, and nine times out of ten are narcissists.

KELLIE-ANNE GALLAGHER

— *'DARING TO SET BOUNDARIES IS ABOUT HAVING THE COURAGE TO LOVE OURSELVES EVEN WHEN WE RISK DISAPPOINTING OTHERS.' – BRENE BROWN*

People's reaction to you setting a boundary to protect your peace is all you need in order to know just how much they care.

If somebody sets about destroying your character, don't get tangled in their low-vibe, negative energy trying to defend yourself. Just walk away... walk away. Don't even bother telling that person they hurt you. There is a pretty good chance this person is a narcissist.

If other people believe their lies, let them. What's done in the darkness always comes into the light. You know your truth, and what anyone thinks of you is none of your business. These people are called their enablers.

These kinds of toxic people know what they're doing. They know exactly how they are hurting you and that's what they want. They don't care, because if they did, they would never treat you like that in the first place.

So please protect your peace like it is the most precious thing in the world.

Do not let guilt or fear or manipulation allow anyone to shit on your beautiful life. No one has power over you.

KELLIE-ANNE GALLAGHER

— 'KARMA IS NOT SOMETHING COMPLICATED OR PHILOSOPHICAL. KARMA MEANS WATCHING YOUR BODY, WATCHING YOUR MOUTH, AND WATCHING YOUR MIND. TRYING TO KEEP THESE THREE DOORS AS PURE AS POSSIBLE IS THE PRACTICE OF KARMA.' — THUBTEN YESHE

DON'T TAKE on other people's lessons and burdens. Be an example and show people how to help themselves. It's not your job to make others see the best in you or to give you the benefit of the doubt. People will see what they want to see, and that reflects where they are in their journey.

The moment you feel sorry for anyone, stop. You don't have to fix their life or situation. Remember, it is their choice to be in this position, it is their lesson to learn. But if someone asks for help, help them within your means to do so. Don't go over the top, otherwise your help is just enabling them. We are all responsible for our own actions. It is their lesson to learn to step aside and let it be.

***

JUST BECAUSE YOU can see an issue with someone does not mean you have to fix it.

Everybody who is in your life should lift you up and love you, value you, and appreciate you for who you are.

Don't take personally how others react and behave. It is a reflection of where they are.

The same goes for friends – you become like the people you hang out with the most.

So if your friends and family, attitudes and behaviours don't reflect your goals and values, then it's time to quietly move on and find people that do. Find the high-vibe, great fun-loving people who have the same interests. They're going to lift you up and help you achieve your dreams.

When it comes to choosing life partners, make sure that the person you choose sees who you are and values you for you; not what they can get from you, not what they can take from you or how they can change you, but what they can bring to the table with you.

It's not about having a perfect relationship. It's about finding someone who matches you and is willing to go through everything without giving up.

* * *

I watched a clip on Instagram that showed the most important question. You should ask a person you want to start a serious relationship with what the worst kind of trauma they have suffered in their life is, and how they dealt with it. You're going to learn quickly how someone deals with conflict, and if they're up for personal growth, they will have reflected on the situation and made a positive out of a negative.

Because the love of your life is going to lift you up and test you in many ways you never thought possible.

Like your children, they are a mirror. They reflect back to you through your conflicts what you need to work on yourself.

FOR YOU, LOVE ME

— *'IF I KNOW WHAT LOVE IS, IT IS BECAUSE OF YOU.'* —
HERMAN HESSE

NEVER FEEL you must stay in a toxic relationship. You don't owe anybody anything. Both of you need to work on becoming better people. Both of you need to want to become better people because if you don't grow together, you grow apart.

There is no point staying in a situation with someone who is unable to self-reflect or want to grow. People show you who they are. Never enter a relationship thinking you're going to fix or change them. You won't.

Protect your relationship. It is precious. Don't let jealousy or fear tear you apart. Lead with love, shower each other in love. Never stop dating. Be grateful for each other and the time you have together. Give each other grace, be kind to each other. You can achieve anything together. Most importantly, love each other as much as you can.

Your relationship with your children is magical. It's your chance to be childlike again. It's your chance to see the beauty and all the small things through the eyes of a child again, and appreciate things we forget about in the busyness of adult life.

FOR YOU, LOVE ME

— *'CHILDREN SEE MAGIC BECAUSE THEY LOOK FOR IT.'* —
CHRISTOPHER MOORE

75

When you have a child, if that's what you decide to do, go with the flow, don't be rigid, don't try and stick to ridiculous schedules. You're only going to make the situation much harder for yourself and so much more difficult than it needs to be.

Children don't stick to rigid schedules. They want to eat when they're hungry. They want to sleep when they're tired. Especially if they are neurodivergent. They want to have fun when they're awake. Just go with the flow.

Teach your child to honour their emotions, let them have the chance to communicate their feelings, wants and needs and genuinely listen to them. As parents, we don't always get it right no matter how much we try. Apologising to them when you are wrong sets an example. What you do for them and how you show up for them leads the way for the future generations. No one has all the answers. Nobody knows your child better than you.

When it comes to your career and relationships, learn to separate them from your personal life. Like they say, don't mix business with pleasure. It helps with work–life balance and it also keeps your friends separate, making things much easier.

* * *

This brings me to forgiveness. If you have conflict in a relationship and you tell that person how they have hurt you, if they truly care about you and the relationship, they won't argue about how they've made you feel. They won't manipulate it to make you feel guilty, and they won't deny what they've done.

FOR YOU, LOVE ME

— PROPER APOLOGIES HAVE THREE PARTS: 1. WHAT I
DID WAS WRONG. 2. I FEEL BADLY THAT I HURT YOU. 3.
HOW DO I MAKE IT BETTER? – RANDY PAUSCH

If they care and they have a willingness for personal growth, they will listen and want to work through the conflict with you. You may not agree on everything, but you will both have the common goal of resolution and peace.

Never waste your time arguing your point of view with someone who isn't emotionally capable of understanding another person's point of view.

Sometimes you have to accept the apology you are never going to get and make peace with that. Forgive them and move on in your own way. Otherwise, if you hold on to the hurt and the injustice, it will manifest as illness in your body.

Mistakes are always forgivable if one has the courage to admit them.

If you have a conflict and you have worked through how you both feel in that situation in a kind, loving and respectful way and an apology has been offered, then forgive and move on. Do not rehash old arguments. Do not waste any more time. Forgiveness means a fresh start – an awesome way to learn how to navigate through conflict.

If you need to apologise, don't delay. Do it and mean it. Say sorry genuinely, let them know you care, then do better next time.

Do not forget to forgive yourself. We are human. We aren't perfect. You aren't always going to get it right, do not beat yourself up over a mistake.

— *FORGIVENESS = FREEDOM*

It's easy to look back and judge yourself in retrospect for things you did in the past, but we didn't know then what we know now. So forgive yourself, be kind to yourself and learn.

WHAT IS NARCISSISTIC PERSONALITY DISORDER, OR NPD?

Narcissistic personality disorder is marked by a grandiose sense of self and a lack of empathy. Unlike other forms of mental illness, narcissism affects a person's very nature and distorts their understanding of themselves. They also affect their relationships and friendships, often resulting in a decreased ability to connect and form healthy bonds with others.

Narcissists have little empathy. They will do, say and manipulate in ways that are unfathomable to normal people. They are cruel, vindictive and have no love for themselves or others. They are deeply disturbed and unhealed individuals who prey on empaths like vampires, sucking the joy and life force from others. They are unable to admit they are anything other than perfect and have deep-seated traumas that need healing. They have suffered childhood trauma and instead of getting better, they get bitter.

WHAT IS AN EMPATH?

An empath has a heightened sense of empathy. They are easily emotionally drained. They have an increased sensitivity to criticism. They avoid conflict. They lack boundaries and often self-isolate. They have a deep sense of feeling different from others. They need lots of time alone to regroup and recharge, and have a history of trauma. They see where others need help and overcompensate for this with their deep understanding and empathy for others' suffering.

While these are lovely abilities to have, unfortunately empaths with unhealed trauma are prey to narcissists, and often think they can fix or heal what they see the narcissist lacks because of their deep sensitivities to others' needs. Empaths need to stop, heal themselves, and remove themselves from the clutches of a narcissist. It's a vicious cycle that can destroy you if you are sucked into a narcissist's darkness. They need your light, your life force, and so you must be vigilant and protective of your light. Leave those who are determined to self-destruct to their own destruction. Create strong, healthy boundaries for behaviour and live your life on your terms.

Be the person who breaks the cycle.

— 'IF YOU WERE JUDGED, CHOOSE UNDERSTANDING. IF YOU WERE REJECTED, CHOOSE ACCEPTANCE. IF YOU WERE SHAMED, CHOOSE COMPASSION. BE THE PERSON YOU NEEDED WHEN YOU WERE HURTING, NOT THE PERSON WHO HURT YOU. VOW TO BE BETTER THAN WHAT BROKE YOU – TO HEAL INSTEAD OF BECOMING BETTER SO YOU CAN ACT FROM YOUR HEART, NOT YOUR PAIN.' – LORI DESCHENE

KELLIE-ANNE GALLAGHER

— *'IF YOU DON'T MANAGE YOUR EMOTIONS, THEN YOUR EMOTIONS WILL MANAGE YOU.' – DOC CHILDRE AND DEBORAH ROZMAN*

EMOTIONS, GROUNDING, MEDITATION

*E*motions are part of the unique experience of being human.
Having ADHD means we may experience our emotions at maximum volume, and sometimes it feels impossible to turn them down.

We lead with our emotions. We make decisions with our emotions. Our emotions decide who we want in our life; who we want to be and where we want to go. They are pivotal to everything. They also are the most important thing in your healing.

Feel your emotions, do not ignore them. Don't try to trap them inside yourself because they make you feel uncomfortable. Sit with them and acknowledge them; feel them and then let them go. This is a big one for a neurodivergent!

Easier said than done when you're in the midst of some really big emotions, but if you hold onto your emotions it's energy that you store inside your body. And if you do not deal with that energy, it can turn into unease, and then your health begins to suffer.

Hello, autistic ADHD meltdowns!

So acknowledge your feelings and emotions; honour them – they are a normal part of being human. Allow yourself a minute to process them and then communicate how you feel.

Can we please break the cycle? Instead of sucking it up or ignoring our emotions, we can communicate and let others help and give you perspective when you are feeling overwhelmed.

Especially boys, please talk about how you feel.

Having ADHD and being on the autism spectrum, and also being an empath means I'm constantly bombarded with so much information that it can be overwhelming.

Sometimes you may need time alone, and that's okay.

If this happens, you need to ground yourself in a way that feels true to you.

FOR YOU, LOVE ME

— 'SPIRITUAL PRACTICE IS NOT JUST SITTING AND MEDITATION. PRACTICE IS LOOKING, THINKING, TOUCHING, DRINKING, EATING, TALKING. EVERY ACT, EVERY BREATH AND EVERY STEP CAN BE PRACTICE AND CAN HELP US TO BECOME MORE OURSELVES.' – NHAT HANH

I'M NOT GOING to tell you that you need to meditate for an hour every day and that you need to pray for an hour every day. Instead, find things that speak truth to you. Is going for a surf the way you calm yourself? Is reading a book soothing for you? Is listening to music relaxing for you? Do what is true for you. Remember, I want you to learn to honour yourself and what you want. It's okay to tell people, 'I'm feeling really big emotions right now and I need to be alone', or 'I need you to let me be for now'.

If you have had sensory overload, shut down and had an autistic meltdown, please be kind to yourself. Don't be too hard on yourself. It's not something you choose to do and it's not something you can switch off. More than likely, you will have little or no recollection of what happened and what you said. So please stop, take a deep breath, and remember you do not choose your meltdowns. Show yourself the kindness and grace you show others. Let others know what happened and ask for help if you need it.

I know I need to remove myself from all noise and lights. I've often hidden in my wardrobe and 'lost it'. It's where I feel safe.

No amount of talking fixes it. I've learnt to feel the emotions; let them pass. A hug and a kiss and lots of reassurance from my husband nurtures me through a meltdown.

My son had lots of meltdowns as a child, and before I was diagnosed, I navigated them quite well as I could relate. Since I was diagnosed, I have managed to avoid complete autistic meltdown myself as there is power in knowledge. I know what's happening now, and it's not as scary. I remove myself from anyone or anything that will trigger it.

Spend some time allowing your system to switch off; to shut down like a computer, so that when it restarts, you're full of energy and able to take on life. Listen to music, get out into nature, get back to basics if everyday life gets too noisy and too busy. Turn off the technology and get back to your true self. Go for a walk, call a friend, go to the beach, ground in nature.

This world is beautiful; go out there and appreciate it. You will feel better for it.

HEALTH

*I*nvest in yourself; it's your greatest asset. Without your health you have nothing.

— *'THE FIRST WEALTH IS HEALTH.'* – RALPH WALDO EMERSON

PRIORITISE GROUNDING, stretching, meditating and exercising. Stress is so destructive, and these practices lower your cortisol levels and allow your body to maintain an alkaline state. Every disease feeds off and acidic, overburdened body.

Neurodivergents need to watch out for 'adrenal burnout'. This can come about from years of stress from masking PTSD, from dealing with your symptoms and people's lack of empathy, using your anxiety to get things done, constantly being stressed, years of negative self-talk, and reliance on caffeine to concentrate. This leaves your cortisol (a stress hormone) levels in overdrive and, if unchecked, you can have a complete nervous breakdown. All these things, plus the toxic relationships I put up with because I thought I had to, led to my nervous breakdown.

When it comes to stress and your health you need to feel your emotions. Don't mask them, avoid them, or run from them. Instead, face them.

If you have had a healthy relationship with healing your past, healing your trauma, and feeling your emotions, you will not feel the need to drink alcohol to unwind at the end of the day or take drugs so that you don't have to think about things that happened to you in the past. Masking a problem can lead to addiction and that leads down a road that is very difficult to get off.

Ultimately, I would love it if you never drank or did drugs. Your body is your temple; the sacred home of your soul. It fights every day to keep you alive against toxins, germs, viruses and your stress.

* * *

I WASN'T aware of just how important eating healthily and exercising was until my health hit rock bottom. If there's anything that I have learnt to be at my optimal health, it is to read all the books by the Medical Medium. That man and the spirit of compassion changed my life; saved my life.

I'm able to enjoy life in a way that I've never been able to. My health is the best it's ever been.

I have found eating a plant-based diet, drinking minimal alcohol and caffeine, and giving up gluten has made me healthier than I have ever been. That is what worked for me. I encourage you to listen to your intuition and discover what works best to nourish your body.

Instead of viewing eating more healthily as being about what you need to cut out and restrict from your diet, think about what you can add for a more nourished body and a fuller life. Drink lemon water in the morning, juice your celery, drink the heavy metal detox smoothie, eat more fruit and take your supplements. It's life-changing.

I'm only sharing what has worked for me, and I hope that it can help you.

FOR YOU, LOVE ME

— *'LET FOOD BE THY MEDICINE AND MEDICINE BE THY FOOD.' – HIPPOCRATES*

I TRULY BELIEVE there's a balance between natural medicine and conventional medicine. Just like Yin and Yang, both are needed at different times. Get your skin checked. Get your heart checked, and check your vitamin levels.

Treat your body like it is your most prized possession.

If you are looking after your car better than yourself, re- prioritise. Your body is your soul's car!

This includes exercising. Find balance; don't go from one extreme to another. Instinctively you know what's right for you and what you can handle.

Exercise because you love your body and you want to honour it by keeping fit. Don't exercise to abuse it and punish it because you had a moment and ate too much chocolate.

PERIODS, PMDD AND PERIMENOPAUSE

These three are a wild ride for the neurodivergent. I didn't get diagnosed until later, but there were signs that were missed. I have severe endometriosis. I told my doctors my periods were hell for me emotionally, not just physically. My emotions around period time were uncontrollable; high highs, low lows, sadness and my rejection sensitivity were out of control. I would have monthly meltdowns, to the point where I didn't recognise myself. Then, the second my period started I was back to being myself. My husband and I would be in shock, like who the hell was that and what just happened? My recurrent miscarriages, IVF and all the hormonal changes made my moods unpredictable. I was doing all the alternative things like meditation, yoga, reiki and cannabidiol oil, but nothing could stop the tsunami of emotions that would hit me.

One GP told me I was depressed and to take antidepressants, but I said it's just one week out of four; I'm not like this all the time. After I was given my diagnosis of premenstrual dysphoric disorder, I deep dived into the information online. How did no one pick up on this earlier?

If this sounds like you, see your GP. The sooner you understand how your body reacts to the hormonal changes that are out of your control, the easier it is on you and your partner and family to navigate the emotions.

* * *

THERE IS a fabulous book called *Soul Speak* by Julia Cannon that explains how emotions trapped in the body and ignoring messages manifest into illness and ailments. Like I said, there is a balance between conventional medicine and healing on a quantum level.

Invest in yourself, invest in your health – it's your most valuable asset.

ROCK BOTTOM

*I*f you have hit your rock bottom, emotionally, physically and spiritually, brace yourself! You are headed for an awakening. Nothing happenings by chance and everything is a lesson. This is a massive shake-up for you. Look at your situation and ask yourself what you need to change to get yourself on the right path.

Try not to learn the hard way!

FOR YOU, LOVE ME

*— ROCK BOTTOM BECAME THE SOLID FOUNDATION ON
WHICH I REBUILT MY LIFE. – J. K. ROWLING*

I HOPE you never hit rock bottom. Not everybody needs to in order to learn their lessons the hard way, and I hope you don't. But if you do, then the only way is up. It's like an arrow shooting you in the right direction.

When I think back to my rock bottom, I realise I missed many signs, that I had no choice but to hit my rock bottom to shake me up and to make me realise that I had to change things – drastically.

My rock bottom came in the form of a near death experience.

What should have been a routine operation for endometriosis removal turned into five-hour surgery, the removal of my appendix and a post-operative infection. When I woke up from that I just knew something wasn't right.

I remember lying on the hospital bed and I didn't know who I was talking to, but I just said out to the universe, 'This is not the way my story ends. I am not going to die. I did not try for ten years to have my son to have it taken away from me'.

And so I got myself out of that hospital and I dedicated my life to learning how to heal myself, physically, mentally and spiritually. It led me on a journey that I would never have gone on had I not hit rock bottom, and now I see how these lessons are necessary to get you back on the right track.

Just know that if you have hit your rock bottom, you are loved, you can get through anything.

This life is a gift. Make the most of it.

FOR YOU, LOVE ME

— *'BECOME AN ALCHEMIST. TRANSMUTE BASE METAL INTO GOLD, SUFFERING INTO CONSCIOUSNESS, DISASTER INTO ENLIGHTENMENT.' – ECKHART TOLLE*

KELLIE-ANNE GALLAGHER

— *'HE WHO HAS OVERCOME HIS FEARS WILL TRULY BE FREE.' – ARISTOTLE.*

FEAR

*H*itting rock bottom leads me to talk about fear. Fear is a unique emotion. It makes you worry about things that nine times out of ten won't happen. Having an ADHD racing car brain means our overthinking leads us to see scary, negative possibilities and it cripples us; it stops us from living the way we should to our fullest potential. It makes you retreat into a dark cave. That's hard to pull yourself out of.

Fear is a lack of love. Fear comes from a lack of love of yourself; from a lack of trust in your judgement, from a lack of trust in the world. If you work on trusting your intuition, if you work on loving yourself, then fear will not control your life. Change your mindset from fright and fear to being open to possibilities. Don't think the worst; think, *what if something wonderful is going to happen?* Say to yourself, *my brain, my emotions are on fast forward. That's okay. That is who I am. But it also means things may not be as bad as I am making them out to be.*

Stop. Pause. Breathe and reevaluate the situation when that fear-based impulsivity tries to kick in.

* * *

IF YOU GET SUCKED into social media and doomsday scrolling and conspiracy theories and it's consuming you and filling you with terror, STOP. Stop chasing that dopamine hit. You won't change anything or help yourself by being bombarded daily by unchecked theories that fill you with terror. Let your social media reflect the kind of energy and life you want. Delete, block and unfollow where necessary.

Fear has its place in your life. It's going to stop you from stepping out in front of a car, or doing something that may potentially hurt you. That's where it's healthy. But if your fear is stopping you from believing in yourself and doing the things that you truly want to do, that's when you need to stop, analyse, and look at why it's overwhelming you.

Don't let the fear of what people think and of what people might say, or what might happen, stop you from doing what you want to do. Hello rejection sensitive dysphoria.

Let that spark of joy ignite when you think of what you want to do or say, or who you love. Lead with that, not with the darkness of what could go wrong what could happen.

What if it all turns out great? Don't live life with regret for the chances that you didn't take and the things that you didn't do, because if the decision is made with love, then there are no regrets. You did the best you could, and that's what it's all about.

Neurodivergents can struggle with fear. Our overactive brains find all sorts of things to fear. Focus on your breath, be calm, and trust your instincts. Success is a series of small victories.

FOR YOU, LOVE ME

— *'FEAR IS A THIEF OF DREAMS.'* - BRIAN KRANS

CAREER, MONEY AND CELEBRATING YOUR WINS

*D*on't get so busy in life that you don't take time to celebrate your wins. Celebrate your achievements, no matter how big or small they are.

THE ATTITUDE OF GRATITUDE

What's the point of all the hard work or dedication to something if you don't stop and enjoy the achievement and the moment of it all?

Here's a way to help you keep a record of your achievements. Each December, buy a journal. Sit down in a quiet place and really think about what your goals are for the year ahead. Write down your three-month, six-month and 12-month goals. Then at the end of that year, reflect on your achievements, your lessons and your blessings.

Become clear about the goals you set and work out your formula to achieve them. It will act as a guidepost, help with direction and keep you on track.

The future belongs to those who believe in the beauty of their dreams.

For example, if you want to buy a house, know exactly how much you need to save, budget accordingly, research the best finance and set yourself a realistic time limit to save. Stay on track and watch how quickly you achieve your goals. It's much better than aimlessly stating what you want without any direction on how to achieve it.

- **Set your goals**
- **Take action**
- **Dreams don't work unless you do**

Everything happens in perfect timing. Be patient and trust the process while you work toward what you want. If you want to be wealthy, then that's fantastic. If you want to travel, or you want to earn enough just to get by, that's fantastic too. Just don't be so busy trying to earn a living that you forget to have a life.

KELLIE-ANNE GALLAGHER

— *'MONEY DOESN'T CHANGE PEOPLE, IT UNMASKS THEM.'* – HENRY FORD

Go out and see this big, beautiful world. Don't let fear stop you from travelling. Obviously, go to places that are safe, but don't let the fear of the unknown stop you from exploring and experiencing everything this life has to offer. Joy is such an important emotion and something that you need to experience daily. Go and do and see and experience everything that brings you joy, whatever that may be. Celebrate achieving this.

Money makes the world go round, no matter how hippy or off-grid you want to be. You still need money to buy food and to eat, so since earning is essential to survival, find a career that brings you joy and is your passion. It will make your life more enjoyable. Even if you must do something that you don't necessarily want to do as a job until you get into your career, it's a small sacrifice to make for a greater reward. Have a plan, have clear goals, and set them in motion.

Being financially independent = freedom.

KELLIE-ANNE GALLAGHER

— *'FAITH IS TAKING THE FIRST STEP, EVEN WHEN YOU DON'T SEE THE WHOLE STAIRCASE.' – MARTIN LUTHER KING JNR*

FAITH

Faith is one of my favourite things to talk about. This is such a personal thing. I cannot tell you what to believe in and I cannot make you believe in anything – or yourself.

This is something that *you* choose to do.

Whatever you have faith in, make sure it is your choice and not out of guilt.

Have faith that you are loved. You have a safe place, you are guided and protected by God, his angels, and your spirit guides.

Have faith in yourself, back yourself.

KELLIE-ANNE GALLAGHER

— 'WE HAVE FAITH IN THE FUTURE IF WE HAVE FAITH IN OURSELVES.' – JOHN F. KENNEDY

FOR YOU, LOVE ME

TO ACHIEVE ALL YOUR DREAMS, have faith that you have all the answers inside yourself.

Listen to yourself, listen to your inner guidance, your intuition.

Have faith that we were created to experience love, joy, peace and good health.

ENJOY LIFE

Be an alchemist and turn any negative into a positive to be grateful, to be happy, and to be loved.

Remember to be kind to yourself. Every day is a step in the right direction.

Have love for yourself and love for others. Be grateful, be positive, and always do the best you can. Keep your mind open. Read and learn as much as you can. Find what is true to you, what speaks to your soul.

Then apply that in your life.

Go out and have fun. See this big, beautiful world. Experience as much as you can, love as much as you can, create as much as you can. Bring beauty, joy and happiness to everyone around you, and most importantly, love.

Love is not what you say. Love is what you do.

LOVE

My favourite topic!
Tell the people you love how much you love them as often as you can.

Love is a doing word. Show love, give love, and receive love.

Radiate love like the sun does light. Love is what makes the world go round. It is the reason you are here; I am here. It is the reason we are going through the experience called life.

There is beauty in everyone and everything.

Love is the highest vibe. It is as essential to the human spirit as air is to the body.

Love and give love, receive love, see love and everything, it is what makes life go on.

God is love. The God energy is love and everything that is created is from love.

Everything manifested is out of love, your love and your desire for that thing, person or place that you want.

KELLIE-ANNE GALLAGHER

— *'LOVE THE LIFE YOU LIVE, LIVE THE LIFE YOU LOVE.'* –
BOB MARLEY

I HAVE an amazing story about manifesting with love.

I discovered the book *The Secret*. I'd heard of it for many years, but I never really thought much about it until one day it spoke to my soul, and I decided to go out and buy it. Looking back, that was when I was ready to hear its message.

If I had read it earlier, I would not have appreciated its message, and it would've been lost on me.

Trust that everything comes to you at the right time.

I read *The Secret*; it was a lightbulb moment.

I thought, *I'm going to try this manifesting thing.*

I had been trying to have a baby for nearly 10 years, and I was feeling like all hope was lost. I had booked to have IVF and then I read *The Secret*, and decided to put it to the test.

I said to the universe, 'I want $26 million or a baby. You pick'.

That night I had a dream that I had won the Lotto and so I raced out on a Saturday and bought a Lotto ticket. I went into the newsagency on Sunday to check the results, and I hadn't won. I was slightly disheartened.

On Monday, my period was one day late, so I took a pregnancy test and guess what? I was pregnant. That was the day I was supposed to start IVF!

I asked, I believed, I received. The universe/God answered my prayer.

I LOVE YOU

My son is way more precious than $26 million, but what a magical way for the universe to show me that manifesting through love can make anything happen.

I am truly grateful for him. He is a gift from God. My son is a miracle and love in human form. He gives my life meaning and purpose. He shows me how to be a better person. He makes me want to be a better person.

Sometimes you will know love and feel the joy and comfort it brings, and then sometimes you will feel alone. It's all a part of the human experience.

Rejection sensitivity can often make you feel deeply alone and question your existence or the meaning of life. But remember that huge, deep emotion you are feeling will pass, things will get better and you will feel love again.

You are loved.

FINAL THOUGHTS...

I am now 40. This is my empowerment era. My time to embrace my age and who I am and what I've learned. When I was younger, I thought 40 was old and that my life would be half over. I was wrong. I feel like it is just beginning, and it's exciting!

I have been through so much in the 39 years leading up to today, especially between my near-death experience in 2017 and my diagnosis in 2023. It was like a fast-tracked shake-up of my life. The beginning of my spiritual journey. It was my awakening.

* * *

I AM proud of my story and my journey of self-discovery. I'm proud of the strength and resilience I have gained. It wasn't easy and I faced many challenges. But I was determined to make every lesson a blessing. To be the alchemist. Turn the negatives into a positive.

I hope that by sharing my story, my inner turmoil and external struggles, it may help you in some way to navigate your neurodivergent life.

Life will present different challenges to you, but that's a part of your story. The challenges you face give you the opportunity to grow. Do not fear the lessons you will face in this life; you have all the answers, determination and all the love you need inside of you. This is your life and it's your choice what you make of it.

* * *

MY DIAGNOSIS and the knowledge that I'm neurodivergent have given me the power of self-acceptance. Understanding how my brain operates has helped me work with my neurodivergence, not against it. I say 'no' to things that bring me discomfort or that I don't want to do, and I finally do not feel guilty for saying 'no' to something or someone.

I now give myself the patience and understanding I had never shown myself before. My inner dialogue is one of love, gratitude and kindness. I no longer dread or fear things like I used to. I embrace my intuition, my hyperfocus and the moments when I need to pause. I focus on my strengths and follow my heart's desires.

I deserve to be here and I'm determined to make my existence meaningful. I am a cycle-breaker; the person in my family who put a stop to passing on toxic intergenerational trauma and behavior.

I unapologetically protect my son and myself. We are surrounded with kindness, honesty and people who love and respect us, and make us feel safe. I don't care what others think. I no longer shrink myself for others' approval; I embrace my uniqueness. I no longer feel the anxiety and burnout that I felt before. I protect my peace and my happiness.

So surround yourself with people who love and value you for you. Who embrace their own healing journey and lift you up instead of putting you down, who own their behavior and want to give you peace and love. Because when you are neurodivergent, no one is harder on you than you are, and you need to be surrounded with patience, kindness, positivity and love that will help you thrive.

The knowledge of my neurodivergence has made me a better wife and mother. I can now articulate what I am feeling and when I am feeling overwhelmed. I can lead by example and help my son navigate his own neurodivergence.

For the first time in my life, I have felt the clarity to ask myself: What do I want? What do I want to do? I am on a spiritual journey, and I want to explore all there is to learn about life.

I realised I want to be an artist. I love to paint. So, guess what? I am. I am enjoying the process of developing my painting style, and doing what I love brings me so much joy. I've given myself permission to call myself an artist, instead of dreading what others think and whether they will like my art, and let go of the rejection-sensitive voice that always whispered in my ear, *who are you kidding, you're not an artist! Stay small and under the radar; that way you won't be judged.*

It's so liberating to finally embrace yourself instead of worrying if you're good enough. I am following my heart and doing what I love.

* * *

THIS IS YOUR LIFE. You deserve to live it on your terms, doing whatever makes you happy. Embrace the uniqueness of how your brain operates. My wish for you, if you are neurodivergent and on your path of self-discovery, is that you find peace, healing and happiness, and that you discover your true purpose – what brings you joy and, most importantly, self-love and acceptance.

To my son

I love you with every fibre of my being. The happiest day of my life was when I found out I was pregnant with you, and then the day I heard your heartbeat, and then the day you came into this world, so please remember I will love you always.

You are my greatest blessing.

To my reader,

I hope you make the most of this beautiful gift of life. I hope your journey is filled with love, the happiest adventures and you achieve everything your heart desires.

Whenever you need a reminder:

'Love is always the answer'.